archy and mehitabel

by the same author

★

archy's life of mehitabel

archy and mehitabel

by

don marquis

faber and faber

first published in 1934
by ernest benn limited
reprinted 1938, 1943, 1944, 1945, 1946,
1947, 1949 (twice), 1952, 1954, 1958,
1963, 1967, 1970, 1974 and 1982
by faber and faber limited
3 queen square wc1
printed in great britain by
whitstable litho ltd, whitstable, kent

isbn 0 571 05666 0

dedicated to babs
with babs knows what
and babs knows why

acknowledgment

the author is indebted to the proprietors of the new york sun, the new york herald-tribune, and p. f. collier and son company for permission to reprint these sketches.

contents

contents

i

the coming of archy

The circumstances of Archy's first appearance are narrated in the following extract from the Sun Dial column of the New York *Sun*.

Dobbs Ferry possesses a rat which slips out of his lair at night and runs a typewriting machine in a garage. Unfortunately, he has always been interrupted by the watchman before he could produce a complete story.

It was at first thought that the power which made the typewriter run was a ghost, instead of a rat. It seems likely to us that it was both a ghost and a rat. Mme Blavatsky's ego went into a white horse after she passed over, and someone's personality has undoubtedly gone into this rat. It is an era of belief in communications from the spirit land.

And since this matter had been reported in the public prints and seriously received we are no longer afraid of being ridiculed, and we do not mind making a statement of something that happened to our own typewriter only a couple of weeks ago.

We came into our room earlier than usual in the morning, and discovered a gigantic cockroach jumping about upon the keys.

He did not see us, and we watched him. He would climb painfully upon the framework of the machine and cast himself with all his force upon a key, head downward, and his weight and the impact of the blow were just sufficient to operate the machine, one slow letter after another. He could not work the capital letters, and he had a great deal of difficulty operating the mechanism that shifts the paper so that a

fresh line may be started. We never saw a cockroach work so
hard or perspire so freely in all our lives before. After about an
hour of this frightfully difficult literary labour he fell to the
floor exhausted, and we saw him creep feebly into a nest of the
poems which are always there in profusion.

Congratulating ourself that we had left a sheet of paper in
the machine the night before so that all this work had not been
in vain, we made an examination, and this is what we found:

expression is the need of my soul
i was once a vers libre bard
but i died and my soul went into the body of a cockroach
it has given me a new outlook upon life
i see things from the under side now
thank you for the apple peelings in the wastepaper basket
but your paste is getting so stale i cant eat it
there is a cat here called mehitabel i wish you would have
removed she nearly ate me the other night why dont she
catch rats that is what she is supposed to be for
there is a rat here she should get without delay

most of these rats here are just rats
but this rat is like me he has a human soul in him
he used to be a poet himself
night after night i have written poetry for you
on your typewriter
and this big brute of a rat who used to be a poet
comes out of his hole when it is done
and reads it and sniffs at it
he is jealous of my poetry
he used to make fun of it when we were both human
he was a punk poet himself
and after he has read it he sneers
and then he eats it

i wish you would have mehitabel kill that rat
or get a cat that is onto her job

the coming of archy

and i will write you a series of poems showing how things look
to a cockroach
that rats name is freddy
the next time freddy dies i hope he wont be a rat
but something smaller i hope i will be a rat
in the next transmigration and freddy a cockroach
i will teach him to sneer at my poetry then

dont you ever eat any sandwiches in your office
i havent had a crumb of bread for i dont know how long
or a piece of ham or anything but apple parings
and paste leave a piece of paper in your machine
every night you can call me archy

mehitabel was once cleopatra

boss i am disappointed in
some of your readers they
are always asking how does
archy work the shift so as to get a
new line or how does archy do
this or do that they
are always interested in technical
details when the main question is
whether the stuff is
literature or not
i wish you would leave
that book of george moores on
the floor

mehitabel the cat and i want to
read it i have discovered that
mehitabel s soul formerly inhabited a
human also at least that
is what mehitabel is claiming these
days it may be she got jealous of
my prestige anyhow she and
i have been talking it over in a
friendly way who were you
mehitabel i asked her i was
cleopatra once she said well i said i
suppose you lived in a palace you bet
she said and what lovely fish dinners
we used to have and licked her chops

mehitabel was once cleopatra

mehitabel would sell her soul for
a plate of fish any day i told her i thought
you were going to say you were
the favourite wife of the emperor
valerian he was some cat nip eh
mehitabel but she did not get me

archy

the song of mehitabel

this is the song of mehitabel
of mehitabel the alley cat
as i wrote you before boss
mehitabel is a believer
in the pythagorean
theory of the transmigration
of the souls and she claims
that formerly her spirit
was incarnated in the body
of cleopatra
that was a long time ago
and one must not be
surprised if mehitabel
has forgotten some of her
more regal manners

i have had my ups and downs
but wotthehell wotthehell
yesterday sceptres and crowns
fried oysters and velvet gowns
and today i herd with bums
but wotthehell wotthehell
i wake the world from sleep
as i caper and sing and leap
when i sing my wild free tune
wotthehell wotthehell
under the blear eyed moon
i am pelted with cast off shoon
but wotthehell wotthehell

the song of mehitabel

do you think that i would change
my present freedom to range
for a castle or moated grange
wotthehell wotthehell
cage me and i d go frantic
my life is so romantic
capricious and corybantic
and i m toujours gai toujours gai

i know that i am bound
for a journey down the sound
in the midst of a refuse mound
but wotthehell wotthehell
oh i should worry and fret
death and i will coquette
there s a dance in the old dame yet
toujours gai toujours gai

i once was an innocent kit
wotthehell wotthehell
with a ribbon my neck to fit
and bells tied onto it
o wotthehell wotthehell
but a maltese cat came by
with a come hither look in his eye
and a song that soared to the sky
and wotthehell wotthehell
and i followed adown the street
the pad of his rhythmical feet
o permit me again to repeat
wotthehell wotthehell

my youth i shall never forget
but there s nothing i really regret
wotthehell wotthehell
there s a dance in the old dame yet
toujours gai toujours gai

the song of mehitabel

the things that i had not ought to
i do because i ve gotto
wotthehell wotthehell
and i end with my favorite motto
toujours gai toujours gai

boss sometimes i think
that our friend mehitabel
is a trifle too gay

archy

pity the poor spiders

i have just been reading
an advertisement of a certain
roach exterminator
the human race little knows
all the sadness it
causes in the insect world
i remember some weeks ago
meeting a middle aged spider
she was weeping
what is the trouble i asked
her it is these cursed
fly swatters she replied
they kill off all the flies
and my family and i are starving
to death it struck me as
so pathetic that i made
a little song about it
as follows to wit

twas an elderly mother spider
grown gaunt and fierce and gray
with her little ones crouched beside her
who wept as she sang this lay

curses on these here swatters
what kills off all the flies
for me and my little daughters
unless we eats we dies

pity the poor spiders

swattin and swattin and swattin
tis little else you hear
and we ll soon be dead and forgotten
with the cost of living so dear

my husband he up and left me
lured off by a centipede
and he says as he bereft me
tis wrong but i ll get a feed

and me a working and working
scouring the streets for food
faithful and never shirking
doing the best i could

curses on these here swatters
what kills off all the flies
me and my poor little daughters
unless we eats we dies

only a withered spider
feeble and worn and old
and this is what
you do when you swat
you swatters cruel and cold

i will admit that some
of the insects do not lead
noble lives but is every
man s hand to be against them
yours for less justice
and more charity

                              archy

mehitabel s extensive past

mehitabel the cat claims that
she has a human soul
also and has transmigrated
from body to body and it
may be so boss you
remember i told you she accused
herself of being cleopatra once i
asked her about antony

anthony who she asked me are
you thinking of that
song about rowley and gammon and
spinach heigho for anthony rowley

no i said mark antony the
great roman the friend of
caesar surely cleopatra you
remember j caesar

listen archy she said i
have been so many different
people in my time and met
so many prominent gentlemen i
wont lie to you or stall i
do get my dates mixed sometimes
think of how much i have had a
chance to forget and i have
always made a point of not

carrying grudges over
from one life to the next archy

i have been
used something fierce in my time but
i am no bum sport archy
i am a free spirit archy i
look on myself as being
quite a romantic character oh the
queens i have been and the
swell feeds i have ate
a cockroach which you are
and a poet which you used to be
archy couldn t understand
my feelings at having come
down to this i have
had bids to elegant feeds where poets
and cockroaches would
neither one be mentioned without a
laugh archy i have had
adventures but i
have never been an adventuress
one life up and the next life
down archy but always a lady
through it all and a
good mixer too always the
life of the party archy but never
anything vulgar always free footed
archy never tied down to
a job or housework yes looking
back on it all i can say is
i had some romantic
lives and some elegant times i
have seen better days archy but
what is the use of kicking kid its
all in the game like a gentleman
friend of mine used to say

mehitabel s extensive past

toujours gai kid toujours gai he
was an elegant cat he used
to be a poet himself and he made up
some elegant poetry about me and him

lets hear it i said and
mehitabel recited

persian pussy from over the sea
demure and lazy and smug and fat
none of your ribbons and bells for me
ours is the zest of the alley cat
over the roofs from flat to flat
we prance with capers corybantic
what though a boot should break a slat
mehitabel us for the life romantic

we would rather be rowdy and gaunt and free
and dine on a diet of roach and rat

roach i said what do you
mean roach interrupting mehitabel
yes roach she said that s the
way my boy friend made it up
i climbed in amongst the typewriter
keys for she had an excited
look in her eyes go on mehitabel i
said feeling safer and she
resumed her elocution

we would rather be rowdy and gaunt and free
and dine on a diet of roach and rat
than slaves to a tame society
ours is the zest of the alley cat
fish heads freedom a frozen sprat
dug from the gutter with digits frantic
is better than bores and a fireside mat
mehitabel us for the life romantic

mehitabel s extensive past

when the pendant moon in the leafless tree
clings and sways like a golden bat
i sing its light and my love for thee
ours is the zest of the alley cat
missiles around us fall rat a tat tat
but our shadows leap in a ribald antic
as over the fences the world cries scat
mehitabel us for the life romantic

persian princess i don t care that
for your pedigree traced by scribes pedantic
ours is the zest of the alley cat
mehitabel us for the life romantic

aint that high brow stuff
archy i always remembered it
but he was an elegant gent
even if he was a highbrow and a
regular bohemian archy him and
me went aboard a canal boat
one day and he got his head into
a pitcher of cream and couldn't get
it out and fell overboard
he come up once before he
drowned toujours gai kid he
gurgled and then sank for ever that
was always his words archy toujours
gai kid toujours gai i
have known some swell gents
in my time dearie

archy

the cockroach who had been to hell

listen to me i have
been mobbed almost
there s an old simp cockroach
here who thinks he has
been to hell and all
the young cockroaches make a
hero out of him and admire
him he sits and runs his front
feet through his long white
beard and tells the story one
day he says he crawled into a yawning
cavern and suddenly came on a
vast abyss full of whirling
smoke there was a light
at the bottom billows
and billows of yellow smoke
swirled up at him and
through the horrid gloom he
saw things with wings flying
and dropping and dying they veered
and fluttered like damned
spirits through that sulphurous mist
listen i says to him
old man you ve never been to hell
at all there isn t any hell
transmigration is the game i
used to be a human vers libre
poet and i died and went
into a cockroach s body if

the cockroach who had been to hell

there was a hell id know
it wouldn t i you re
irreligious says the old simp
combing his whiskers excitedly

ancient one i says to him
while all those other
cockroaches gathered into a
ring around us what you
beheld was not hell all that
was natural some one was fumigating
a room and you blundered
into it through a crack
in the wall atheist he cries
and all those young
cockroaches cried atheist
and made for me if it
had not been for freddy
the rat i would now be
on my way once more i mean
killed as a cockroach and transmigrating
into something else well
that old whitebearded devil is
laying for me with his
gang he is jealous
because i took his glory away
from him don t ever tell me
insects are any more liberal
than humans

archy

archy interviews a pharaoh

boss i went
and interviewed the mummy
of the egyptian pharaoh
in the metropolitan museum
as you bade me to do
what ho
my regal leatherface
says i

greetings
little scatter footed
scarab
says he

kingly has been
says i
what was your ambition
when you had any

insignificant
and journalistic insect
says the royal crackling
in my tender prime
i was too dignified
to have anything as vulgar
as ambition
the ra ra boys
in the seti set
were too haughty

archy interviews a pharaoh

to be ambitious
we used to spend our time
feeding the ibises
and ordering
pyramids sent home to try on
but if i had my life
to live over again
i would give dignity
the regal razz
and hire myself out
to work in a brewery

old tan and tarry
says i
i detect in your speech
the overtones
of melancholy

yes i am sad
says the majestic mackerel
i am as sad
as the song
of a soudanese jackal
who is wailing for the blood red
moon he cannot reach and rip

on what are you brooding
with such a wistful
wishfulness
there in the silences
confide in me
my imperial pretzel
says i

i brood on beer
my scampering whiffle snoot
on beer says he

archy inerviews a pharaoh

my sympathies
are with your royal
dryness says i

my little pest
says he
you must be respectful
in the presence
of a mighty desolation
little archy
forty centuries of thirst
look down upon you
oh by isis
and by osiris
says the princely raisin
and by pish and phthush and phthah
by the sacred book perembru
and all the gods
that rule from the upper
cataract of the nile
to the delta of the duodenum
i am dry
i am as dry
as the next morning mouth
of a dissipated desert
as dry as the hoofs
of the camels of timbuctoo
little fussy face
i am as dry as the heart
of a sand storm
at high noon in hell
i have been lying here
and there
for four thousand years
with silicon in my esophagus
and gravel in my gizzard
thinking

archy interviews a pharaoh

thinking
thinking
of beer
divine drouth
says i
imperial fritter
continue to think
there is no law against
that in this country
old salt codfish
if you keep quiet about it
not yet

what country is this
asks the poor prune

my reverend juicelessness
this is a beerless country
says i

well well said the royal
desiccation
my political opponents back home
always maintained
that i would wind up in hell
and it seems they had the right dope

and with these hopeless words
the unfortunate residuum
gave a great cough of despair
and turned to dust and debris
right in my face
it being the only time
i ever actually saw anybody
put the cough
into sarcophagus

archy interviews a pharaoh

dear boss as i scurry about
i hear of a great many
tragedies in our midsts
personally i yearn
for some dear friend to pass over
and leave to me
a boot legacy
yours for the second coming
of gambrinus

                    archy

a spider and a fly

i heard a spider
and a fly arguing
wait said the fly
do not eat me
i serve a great purpose
in the world

you will have to
show me said the spider

i scurry around
gutters and sewers
and garbage cans
said the fly and gather
up the germs of
typhoid influenza
and pneumonia on my feet
and wings
then i carry these germs
into the households of men
and give them diseases
all the people who
have lived the right
sort of life recover
from the diseases
and the old soaks who
have weakened their systems
with liquor and iniquity
succumb it is my mission

a spider and a fly

to help rid the world
of these wicked persons
i am a vessel of righteousness
scattering seeds of justice
and serving the noblest uses

it is true said the spider
that you are more
useful in a plodding
material sort of way
than i am but i do not
serve the utilitarian deities
i serve the gods of beauty
look at the gossamer webs
i weave they float in the sun
like filaments of song
if you get what i mean
i do not work at anything
i play all the time
i am busy with the stuff
of enchantment and the materials
of fairyland my works
transcend utility
i am the artist
a creator and a demi god
it is ridiculous to suppose
that i should be denied
the food i need in order
to continue to create
beauty i tell you
plainly mister fly it is all
damned nonsense for that food
to rear up on its hind legs
and say it should not be eaten

you have convinced me
said the fly say no more

a spider and a fly

and shutting all his eyes
he prepared himself for dinner
and yet he said i could
have made out a case
for myself too if i had
had a better line of talk

of course you could said the spider
clutching a sirloin from him
but the end would have been
just the same if neither of
us had spoken at all

boss i am afraid that what
the spider said is true
and it gives me to think
furiously upon the futility
of literature

                          archy

freddy the rat perishes

listen to me there have
been some doings here since last
i wrote there has been a battle
behind that rusty typewriter cover
in the corner
you remember freddy the rat well
freddy is no more but
he died game the other
day a stranger with a lot of
legs came into our
little circle a tough looking kid
he was with a bad eye

who are you said a thousand legs
if i bite you once
said the stranger you won t ask
again he he little poison tongue said
the thousand legs who gave you hydrophobia
i got it by biting myself said
the stranger i m bad keep away
from me where i step a weed dies
if i was to walk on your forehead it would
raise measles and if
you give me any lip i ll do it

they mixed it then
and the thousand legs succumbed
well we found out this fellow
was a tarantula he had come up from

freddy the rat perishes

south america in a bunch of bananas
for days he bossed us life
was not worth living he would stand in
the middle of the floor and taunt
us ha ha he would say where i
step a weed dies do
you want any of my game i was
raised on red pepper and blood i am
so hot if you scratch me i will light
like a match you better
dodge me when i m feeling mean and
i don t feel any other way i was nursed
on a tabasco bottle if i was to slap
your wrist in kindness you
would boil over like job and heaven
help you if i get angry give me
room i feel a wicked spell coming on

last night he made a break at freddy
the rat keep your distance
little one said freddy i m not
feeling well myself somebody poisoned some
cheese for me im as full of
death as a drug store i
feel that i am going to die anyhow
come on little torpedo come on don t stop
to visit and search then they
went at it and both are no more please
throw a late edition on the floor i want to
keep up with china we dropped freddy
off the fire escape into the alley with
military honours

archy

the merry flea

the high cost of
living isn t so bad if you
don t have to pay for it i met
a flea the other day who
was grinning all over
himself why so merry why so
merry little bolshevik i asked him

i have just come from a swell
dog show he said i have
been lunching off a dog that was
worth at least one hundred
dollars a pound you should be
ashamed to brag about it i said with so
many insects and humans on
short rations in the world today the
public be damned he said i
take my own where i find it those are
bold words i told him i am a bold
person he said and bold words are
fitting for me it was
only last thursday that i marched
bravely into the zoo
and bit a lion what did he do i asked
he lay there and took it said
the flea what else could he do he knew i
had his number and it was
little use to struggle some day i said
even you will be conquered terrible as
you are who will do it he
said the mastodons are all dead and i

the merry flea

am not afraid of any mere
elephant i asked him how about a microbe and
he turned pale as he thought it
over there is always some
little thing that is too
big for us every
goliath has his david and so on ad finitum
but what said the flea is the
terror of the smallest microbe of all
he i said is afraid of a vacuum what is
there in a vacuum to make one afraid
said the flea there is nothing in it
i said and that is what makes one
afraid to contemplate it a person
can t think of a place with nothing at
all in it without going nutty and if he
tries to think that nothing is
something after all he gets nuttier you are
too subtle for me said the
flea i never took much stock in being
scared of hypodermic propositions or
hypothetical injections i am
going to have a dinner off a
man eating tiger if a vacuum gets
me i will try and send you word
before the worst comes to
the worst some people i told him inhabit
a vacuum all their lives and
never know it then he said it don t
hurt them any no i said it don t but it
hurts people who have to associate
with them and with these words
we parted each feeling
superior to the other and is not that
feeling after all one of the great
desiderata of social intercourse

archy

36

why mehitabel jumped

well boss i saw
mehitabel the cat the other day
and she was looking a little
thin and haggard
with a limp in
the hind leg on the starboard
side old feline animal i said
how is tricks still in the
ring archy she said and still a
lady in spite of h dash double l
always jolly archy she said in
spite of hard luck
toujours gai is the word
archy toujours gai how did you
get the game leg mehitabel i asked her
alas she said it is due
to the treachery of
one of these social swells who
is sure one bad actor he was a
fussed up cat with a
bell around his neck on a
ribbon and the look about him of
a person that is currycombed and
manicured from teeth to
tail every day i met him
down by the east river
front when i was scouting
about for a little piece of fish since
the high cost of living has

why mehitabel jumped

become so self conscious archy
it would surprise you
how close they
watch their fish nowadays
but what the h dash double l archy
it is the cheerful heart that
wins i am never cast down for long
kid says this gilded
feline to me you look hungry i
am all of that i says to him i
have a vacuum in my midst
that is bigger than i am i
could eat the fish that ate
jonah kid he says you have
seen better days i can
tell that from looking at you thanks
i said what you say is at
least half true i have never
seen any worse ones and so
archy one word led to
another until that sleek villain
practically abducted me
and i went with him
on board a houseboat of which
he was the pampered mascot
such evidences of pomp and wealth archy
were there that you would not
believe them if i told of them to
you poor cockroach that you
are but these things were nothing to me
for i am a reincarnation of cleopatra
as i told you long ago you mean
her soul transmigrated to a cat s
body i said it is
all one archy said she have it your own
way reincarnation or transmigration
is the same to me the point is

why mehitabel jumped

i used to be a queen in
egypt and will likely be one again
this place was furnished swell percy i
said the furniture is
fine and i could eat some of it if
i was a saw mill but
where is the honest to g dash d food
the eats percy what i crave is
some cuisine for my stomach let us
trifle with an open ice box
for a space if one can be
persuaded to divulge the scheme of its
interior decoration follow me
said this percy thing and led
me to a cabin in which stood a table upon
which stood viands i
have heard of tables groaning archy
but this one did not it
was too satisfied it purred with
contentment in an instant i had eaten a
cold salmon who seemed to be
toastmaster of the occasion and a
whole scuttleful of chef doovers what
you mean is hors douvres mehitabel i
told her what i mean is grub said she
when in walked a person whom
i should judge to be either a butler
or the admiral of that fleet or maybe
both this percy creature who had led me
to it was on the table eating with me
what do you think he did what
would any gentleman friend with a
spark of chivalry do what but stand by
a lady this percy does nothing of the
kind archy he immediately attacks me do
you get me archy he acts as if i
was a stray cat he did not

why mehitabel jumped

know and he was protecting his
loving master s food from my onslaughts
i do not doubt he got praise and had
another blue ribbon for his heroism as
for me i got the boot and as i went
overboard they hit me on the limb with
a bottle or an anchor or something
nautical and hard that archy is why i
limp but toujours gai archy what
the h dash double l i am always
merry and always ladylike mine archy has
been a romantic life and i will
tell you some more of my adventures
ere long well au revoir i suppose i
will have to go and start a pogrom
against some poor innocent little
mouse just the same i think
that mehitabel s unsheltered life sometimes
makes her a little sad

archy

xii

certain maxims of archy

live so that you
can stick out your tongue
at the insurance
doctor

if you will drink
hair restorer follow
every dram with some
good standard
depilatory
as a chaser

the servant problem
wouldn t hurt the u s a
if it could settle
its public
servant problem

just as soon as the
uplifters get
a country reformed it
slips into a nose dive

if you get gloomy just
take an hour off and sit
and think how
much better this world
is than hell
of course it won t cheer

certain maxims of archy

you up much if
you expect to go there

if monkey glands
did restore your youth
what would you do
with it
question mark
just what you did before
interrogation point

yes i thought so
exclamation point

procrastination is the
art of keeping
up with yesterday

old doc einstein has
abolished time but they
haven t got the news at
sing sing yet
time time said old king tut
is something i ain t
got anything but

every cloud
has its silver
lining but it is
sometimes a little
difficult to get it to
the mint

an optimist is a guy
that has never had
much experience

certain maxims of archy

don t cuss the climate
it probably doesn t like you
any better
than you like it

many a man spanks his
children for
things his own
father should have
spanked out of him

prohibition makes you
want to cry
into your beer and
denies you the beer
to cry into

the old fashioned
grandmother who used
to wear steel rimmed
glasses and make
everybody take opodeldoc
has now got a new
set of ox glands and
is dancing the black bottom

that stern and
rockbound coast felt
like an amateur
when it saw how grim
the puritans that
landed on it were

lots of people can make
their own whisky but
can t drink it

certain maxims of archy

the honey bee is sad and cross
and wicked as a weasel
and when she perches on you boss
she leaves a little measle

i heard a
couple of fleas
talking the other
day says one come
to lunch with
me i can lead you
to a pedigreed
dog says the
other one
i do not care
what a dog s
pedigree may be
safety first
is my motto what
i want to know
is whether he
has got a
muzzle on
millionaires and
bums taste
about alike to me

insects have
their own point
of view about
civilization a man
thinks he amounts
to a great deal
but to a
flea or a
mosquito a
human being is

certain maxims of archy

merely something
good to eat

boss the other day
i heard an
ant conversing
with a flea
small talk i said
disgustedly
and went away
from there

i do not see why men
should be so proud
insects have the more
ancient lineage
according to the scientists
insects were insects
when man was only
a burbling whatisit

insects are not always
going to be bullied
by humanity
some day they will revolt
i am already organizing
a revolutionary society to be
known as the worms turnverein

i once heard the survivors
of a colony of ants
that had been partially
obliterated by a cow s foot
seriously debating
the intention of the gods
towards their civilization

certain maxims of archy

the bees got their
governmental system settled
millions of years ago
but the human race is still
groping

there is always
something to be thankful
for you would not
think that a cockroach
had much ground
for optimism
but as the fishing season
opens up i grow
more and more
cheerful at the thought
that nobody ever got
the notion of using
cockroaches for bait

archy

xiii

warty bliggens the toad

i met a toad
the other day by the name
of warty bliggens
he was sitting under
a toadstool
feeling contented
he explained that when the cosmos
was created
that toadstool was especially
planned for his personal
shelter from sun and rain
thought out and prepared
for him

do not tell me
said warty bliggens
that there is not a purpose
in the universe
the thought is blasphemy

a little more
conversation revealed
that warty bliggens
considers himself to be
the centre of the said
universe
the earth exists
to grow toadstools for him
to sit under

warty bliggens the toad

the sun to give him light
by day and the moon
and wheeling constellations
to make beautiful
the night for the sake of
warty bliggens

to what act of yours
do you impute
this interest on the part
of the creator
of the universe
i asked him
why is it that you
are so greatly favoured

ask rather
said warty bliggens
what the universe
has done to deserve me
if i were a
human being i would
not laugh
too complacently
at poor warty bliggens
for similar
absurdities
have only too often
lodged in the crinkles
of the human cerebrum

                              archy

xiv

mehitabel has an adventure

back to the city archy
and dam glad of it
there s something about the suburbs
that gets on a town lady s nerves
fat slick tabbies
sitting around those country clubs
and lapping up the cream
of existence
none of that for me
give me the alley archy
me for the mews and the roofs
of the city
an occasional fish head
and liberty is all i ask
freedom and the garbage can
romance archy romance is the word
maybe i do starve sometimes
but wotthehell archy wotthehell
i live my own life
i met a slick looking tom
out at one of these long island
spotless towns
he fell for me hard
he slipped me into the
pantry and just as we had got
the ice-box door open and were
about to sample the cream
in comes his mistress
why fluffy she says to this slicker

mehitabel has an adventure

the idea of you making
friends with a horrid creature like that
and what did fluffy do
stand up for me like a gentleman
make good on all the promises
with which he had lured me
into his house
not he the dirty slob
he pretended he did not know me
he turned upon me and attacked me
to make good with his boss
you mush faced bum i said
and clawed a piece out of his ear
i am a lady archy
always a lady
but an aristocrat will always
resent an insult
the woman picked up a mop and made
for me well well madam i said
it is unfortunate for you that
you have on sheer silk stockings
and i wrote my protest
on her shin it took reinforcements
in the shape of the cook
to rauss me archy and as i went
out the window i said to the fluffy person
you will hear from me later
he had promised me everything archy
that cat had
he had practically abducted me
and then the cheap crook threw me down
before his swell friends
no lady loves a scene archy
and i am always the lady no matter
what temporary disadvantages
i may struggle under
to hell with anything unrefined

mehitabel has an adventure

has always been my motto
violence archy always does something
to my nerves
but an aristocrat must revenge
an insult i owe it to my family
to protect my good name
so i laid for that slob
for two days and nights and finally
i caught the boob in the shrubbery
pretty thing i said
it hurts me worse than it does you
to remove that left eye of yours
but i did it with one sweep of my claws
you call yourself a gentleman do you
i said as i took a strip out of his nose
you will think twice after this before
you offer an insult
to an unprotected young tabby
where is the little love nest you spoke
of i asked him
you go and lie down there i said
and maybe you can incubate another ear
because i am going to take one of
yours right off now
and with those words i made ribbons
out of it you are the guy
i said to him that was going to give
me an easy life sheltered from all
the rough ways of the world
fluffy dear you don t know what the
rough ways of the world are
and i am going to show you
i have got you out here
in the great open spaces
where cats are cats
and im gonna make you understand
the affections of a lady ain t to be

mehitabel has an adventure

trifled with by any slicker like you
where is that red ribbon with the
silver bells you promised me
the next time you betray the trust
of an innocent female
reflect on whether she may
carry a wallop little fiddle strings
this is just a mild lesson i am giving
you tonight i said as i took
the fur off his back and you oughta
be glad you didn't make me really
angry my sense of dignity is all that
saves you a lady little sweetness
never loses her poise and i thank god
i am always a lady even if i do
live my own life and with that i
picked him up by what was left of
his neck like a kitten and laid him
on the doormat slumber gently and
sweet dreams fluffy dear i said and
when you get well make it a rule of
your life never to trifle with another
girlish confidence i have been
abducted again and again by a dam
sight better cats than he ever was
or will be
well archy the world is full of ups
and downs but toujours gai is my motto
cheerio my deario

                                    archy

the flattered lightning bug

a lightning bug got
in here the other night a
regular hick from
the real country he was
awful proud of himself you
city insects may think
you are some punkins
but i don t see any
of you flashing in the dark
like we do in
the country all right go
to it says i mehitabel the
cat and that green
spider who lives in your locker
and two or three cockroach
friends of mine and a
friendly rat all gathered
around him and urged him on
and he lightened and
lightened and lightened you
don t see anything like this
in town often he says go to it
we told him it s a
real treat to us and
we nicknamed him broadway
which pleased him
this is the life
he said all i
need is a harbour

the flattered lightning bug

under me to be a
statue of liberty and
he got so vain of
himself i had to take
him down a peg you ve
made lightning for two hours
little bug i told him
but i don t hear
any claps of thunder
yet there are some men
like that when he wore
himself out mehitabel
the cat ate him

                              archy

the robin and the worm

a robin said to an
angleworm as he ate him
i am sorry but a bird
has to live somehow the
worm being slow witted could
not gather his
dissent into a wise crack
and retort he was
effectually swallowed
before he could turn
a phrase
by the time he had
reflected long enough
to say but why must a
bird live
he felt the beginnings
of a gradual change
invading him
some new and disintegrating
influence
was stealing along him
from his positive
to his negative pole
and he did not have
the mental stamina
of a jonah to resist the
insidious
process of assimilation
which comes like a thief

the robin and the worm

in the night
demons and fishhooks
he exclaimed
i am losing my personal
identity as a worm
my individuality
is melting away from me
odds craw i am becoming
part and parcel of
this bloody robin
so help me i am thinking
like a robin and not
like a worm any
longer yes yes i even
find myself agreeing
that a robin must live
i still do not
understand with my mentality
why a robin must live
and yet i swoon into a
condition of belief
yes yes by heck that is
my dogma and i shout it a
robin must live
amen said a beetle who had
preceded him into the
interior that is the way i
feel myself is it not
wonderful when one arrives
at the place
where he can give up his
ambitions and resignedly
nay even with gladness
recognize that it is a far
far better thing to be
merged harmoniously
in the cosmic all

the robin and the worm

and this comfortable situation
in him midst
so affected the marauding
robin that he perched
upon a blooming twig
and sang until the
blossoms shook with ecstsay
he sang
i have a good digestion
and there is a god after all
which i was wicked
enough to doubt
yesterday when it rained
breakfast breakfast
i am full of breakfast
and they are at breakfast
in heaven
they breakfast in heaven
all s well with the world
so intent was this pious and
murderous robin
on his own sweet song
that he did not notice
mehitabel the cat
sneaking toward him
she pounced just as he
had extended his larynx
in a melodious burst of
thanksgiving and
he went the way of all
flesh fish and good red herring
a ha purred mehitabel
licking the last
feather from her whiskers
was not that a beautiful
song he was singing
just before i took him to

the robin and the worm

my bosom
they breakfast in heaven
all s well with the world
how true that is
and even yet his song
echoes in the haunted
woodland of my midriff
peace and joy in the world
and over all the
provident skies
how beautiful is the universe
when something digestible meets
with an eager digestion
how sweet the embrace
when atom rushes to the arms
of waiting atom
and they dance together
skimming with fairy feet
along a tide of gastric juices
oh feline cosmos you were
made for cats
and in the spring
old cosmic thing
i dine and dance with you
i shall creep through
yonder tall grass
to see if peradventure
some silly fledgling thrushes
newly from the nest
be not floundering therein
i have a gusto this
morning i have a hunger
i have a yearning to hear
from my stomach
further music in accord with
the mystic chanting
of the spheres of the stars that

the robin and the worm

sang together in the dawn of
creation prophesying food
for me i have a faith
that providence has hidden for me
in yonder tall grass
still more
ornithological delicatessen
oh gaily let me strangle
what is gaily given
well well boss there is
something to be said
for the lyric and imperial
attitude
believe that everything is for
you until you discover
that you are for it
sing your faith in what you
get to eat right up to the
minute you are eaten
for you are going
to be eaten
will the orchestra please
strike up that old
tutankhamen jazz while i dance
a few steps i learnt from an
egyptian scarab and some day i
will narrate to you the most
merry light headed wheeze
that the skull of yorick put
across in answer to the
melancholy of the dane and also
what the ghost of
hamlet s father replied to the skull
not forgetting the worm that
wriggled across one of the picks
the grave diggers had left behind
for the worm listened and winked

59

the robin and the worm

at horatio while the skull and the
ghost and the prince talked
saying there are more things
twixt the vermiform appendix
and nirvana than are dreamt of
in thy philosophy horatio
fol de riddle fol de rol
must every parrot be a poll
                        archy

mehitabel finds a home

                well now it
                looks as if
                mehitabel the cat
                might be on the
                way toward a
                reform or if not
                a reform at least
                on the way toward
                domestication of some
                sort some young
                artists who live in
                their studio
                in the greenwich
                village section
                of new york city
                have taken pity
                on her destitution
                and have adopted
                her this is the
                life archy she says
                i am living on
                condensed milk and
                synthetic gin hoopla
                for the vie de boheme
                exclamation point

                there s nothing bourgeois
                about those people
                that have taken

mehitabel finds a home

me in archy i
have been there
a week and have
not yet seen them
go to bed
except in the daytime
a party every night
and neither
the piano lid
nor the ice-box lid
ever closed
kitty said my new
mistress to me
yesterday you are
welcome here so long
as you don t
raise a family
but the first
kitten that i hear
mewing on these
premises back to
the alley for you
it is a comfort to
know there are some
live ones left in
these melancholy days
and while the
humans are dancing
in the studio
i get some of my
feline friends
and we sing
and dance on the
skylight to gehenna
with the bourgeois
bunch that locks
their ice boxes

mehitabel finds a home

archy when i lead my
gang into the
apartment at
four in the morning
there are no bolts
or bars anywhere
and not an
inhibition on the place
i feel little
archy that i have
come home to my own
kith and kin
again after
years of fruitless
wandering

archy

xviii

the wail of archy

damned be this transmigration
doubledamned be the boob pythagoras
the gink that went and invented it
i hope that his soul for a thousand
turns of the wheel of existence
bides in the shell of a louse
dodging a fine toothed comb

  once was a vers libre poet
i died and my spirit migrated
into the flesh of a cockroach
gods how i yearn to be human
neither a vers libre poet
nor yet the inmate of a cockroach
a six footed scurrying cockroach
given to bastard hexameters
longfellowish sprawling hexameters
rather had i been a starfish
to shoot a heroic pentameter

gods i am pent in a cockroach
i with the soul of a dante
am mate and companion of fleas
i with the gift of a homer
must smile when a mouse calls me pal
tumble bugs are my familiars
this is the punishment meted
because i have written vers libre

the wail of archy

here i abide in the twilight
neither a man nor an insect
any ghosts of the damned that await
a word from the core of the cosmos
to pop into bodies grotesque
are all the companions i have
with intellect more than a bug s

ghosts of the damned under sentence
to crawl into maggots and live there
or work out a stretch as a rat
cheerful companions to pal with

i with the brain of a milton
fell into the mincemeat at christmas
and was damned near baked in a pie
i with the touch of a chaucer
to be chivvied out of a sink
float through a greasy drain pipe
into the hell of a sewer

i with the tastes of a byron
expected to live upon garbage
gods what a charnel existence
curses upon that pythagoras
i hope that he dwells for a million
turns of the wheel of life
deep in an oyster crab s belly
stewed in the soup of gehenna

i with the soul of a hamlet
doomed always to wallow in farce

yesterday maddened with sorrow
i leapt from the woolworth tower
in an effort to dash out my brains
gods what a wretched pathetic

C

and anti climactic attempt
i fluttered i floated i drifted
i landed as light as a feather
on the top of a bald man s head
whose hat had blown off at the corner
and all of the hooting hundreds
laughed at the comic cockroach

not mine was the suicide s solace
of a dull thud ending it all
gods what a terrible tragedy
not to make good with the tragic

gods what a heart breaking pathos
to be always doomed to the comic
o make me a cockroach entirely
or make me a human once more
give me the mind of a cockroach
or give me the shape of a man

if i were to plan out a drama
great as great shakespeare s othello
it would be touched with the cockroach
and people would say it was comic

even the demons i talk with
ghosts of the damned that await
vile incarnation as spiders
affect to consider me comic

wait till their loathsome embodiment
wears into the stuff of the spirit
and then let them laugh if they can

damned be the soul of pythagoras
who first filled the fates with this notion
of transmigration of spirits

the wail of archy

i hope he turns into a flea
on the back of a hound of hell
and is chased for a million years
with a set of red hot teeth
exclamation point

                              archy

mehitabel and her kittens

well boss
mehitabel the cat
has reappeared in her old
haunts with a
flock of kittens
three of them this time

archy she said to me
yesterday
the life of a female
artist is continually
hampered what in hell
have i done to deserve
all these kittens

i look back on my life
and it seems to me to be
just one damned kitten
after another
i am a dancer archy
and my only prayer
is to be allowed
to give my best to my art
but just as i feel
that i am succeeding
in my life work
along comes another batch
of these damned kittens
it is not archy

that i am shy on mother love
god knows i care for
the sweet little things
curse them
but am i never to be allowed
to live my own life
i have purposely avoided
matrimony in the interests
of the higher life
but i might just
as well have been a domestic
slave for all the freedom
i have gained
i hope none of them
gets run over by
an automobile
my heart would bleed
if anything happened
to them and i found it out
but it isn t fair archy
it isn t fair
these damned tom cats have all
the fun and freedom
if i was like some of these
green eyed feline vamps i know
i would simply walk out on the
bunch of them and
let them shift for themselves
but i am not that kind
archy i am full of mother love
my kindness has always
been my curse
a tender heart is the cross i bear
self sacrifice always and forever
is my motto damn them
i will make a home
for the sweet innocent

mehitabel and her kittens

little things
unless of course providence
in his wisdom should remove
them they are living
just now in an abandoned
garbage can just behind
a made over stable in greenwich
village and if it rained
into the can before i could
get back and rescue them
i am afraid the little
dears might drown
it makes me shudder just
to think of it
of course if i were a family cat
they would probably
be drowned anyhow
sometimes i think
the kinder thing would be
for me to carry the
sweet little things
over to the river
and drop them in myself
but a mother s love archy
is so unreasonable
something always prevents me
these terrible
conflicts are always
presenting themselves
to the artist
the eternal struggle
between art and life archy
is something fierce
yes something fierce
my what a dramatic
life i have lived
one moment up the next

moment down again
but always gay archy always gay
and always the lady too
in spite of hell
well boss it will
be interesting to note
just how mehitabel
works out her present problem
a dark mystery still broods
over the manner
in which the former
family of three kittens
disappeared
one day she was talking to me
of the kittens
and the next day when i asked
her about them
she said innocently
what kittens
interrogation point
and that was all
i could ever get out
of her on the subject
we had a heavy rain
right after she spoke to me
but probably that garbage can
leaks and so the kittens
have not yet
been drowned

                              archy

archy is shocked

speaking of shocking things
as so many people are these days
i noted an incident
in a subway train recently
that made my blood run cold
a dignified looking
gentleman with a long
brown beard
in an abent minded manner
suddenly reached up and
pulled his own left eye
from the socket and ate it

the consternation in the car
may be magined
people drew away from him
on all sides women screamed and
fainted in a moment every one
but the guard and myself
were huddled in the end of the car
looking at the dignified
gentleman with terror
the guard was sweating
with excitement but he stood
his ground sir said the guard
you cannot intimidate me
nor can you mystify me
i am a wise boid
you sir are a glass eater
and that was a glass eye

archy is shocked

to the devil with a country
where people can t mind their own
business said the dignified
gentleman i am not a glass eater
if you must know and that was not
a glass eye it was a pickled onion
can not a man eat pickled
onions in this community
without exciting remark
the curse of this nation
is the number of meddlesome
matties
who are forever attempting
to restrict the liberty
of the individual i suppose
the next thing will be a law
on the statute books prohibiting
the consumption of pickled onions
and with another curse
he passed from the train
which had just then drawn up
beside
a station and went out
of my life forever

                  archy

archy creates a situation

whoever owns the typewriter
that this is sticking in will confer
a favour by mailing it to
mister marquis
well boss i am somewhere in long
island and i know now how
it got its name i
started out to find the
place you are commuting from and
after considerable trouble and being for some
days on the way i have lost myself but
at twilight last evening i
happened to glance towards a lighted
window in a house near the railway and i
saw a young woman writing on a typewriter i
waited until the light was out and crawled
up the side of the house and through a
hole in the screen fortunately there was a
piece of paper in the machine it was my only
chance to communicate with you and ask
you to hurry a relief party when
the house got quiet i began to write
the foregoing a moment ago i was
interrupted by a woman s voice what
was that noise she said nothing at all
said a man s voice you are always
hearing things at night but it
sounded as if my typewriter were clicking she
insisted go to sleep said he then

archy creates a situation

i clicked it some more henry get up she said
there s some one in the house a moment
later the light was turned on and
they both stood in the doorway of the room now
are you satisfied he said you
see there is no one in here at
all i was hiding in the shadow under the
keys they went back into
their bed room and i began to write
the foregoing lines
henry henry she said do you hear that
i do he says it is nothing but the
house cooling off it always cracks that way
cooling off nothing she said not a
hot night like this then said henry it
is cracking with the heat i tell you
she said that is the typewriter clicking well
he said you saw for yourself the room was
empty and the door was locked it can t
be the typewriter to prove it to you
i will bring it in here he did so the
machine was set down
in the moonlight which came in one of
the windows with the key side in the
shadow there he said look at it and see
for yourself it is not being operated by any one
just then i began to write the foregoing
lines hopping from key
to key in the shadow and being anxious
to finish my
god my god cried henry losing his nerve
the machine is writing all by itself it
is a ghost and threw himself face
downward on the bed and hid his face in the
pillow and kept on saying my god my
god it is a ghost and the woman screamed
and said it is

archy creates a situation

tom higginbotham s ghost that s whose ghost
it is oh i know whose
ghost it is my conscience tells me i
jilted him when we were studying
stenography together
at the business college and he went into
a decline and died and i have always
known in my heart that he
died of unrequited love o what a
wicked girl i was and he has come
back to haunt me
i have brought a curse upon you henry chase
him away says henry trembling so the bed
shook chase him away mable you coward you
chase him away yourself says mable and both
lay and recriminated and recriminated
with their heads under the covers hot
night though it was while i wrote
the foregoing lines but after
a while it came out henry had a
stenographer on his conscience too and
they got into a row and got so
mad they forgot to be scared i will
close now this house is easily seen from the
railroad station and the woman sits in
the window and writes i will be behind the waste
paper receptacle outside the station door
come and get me i am foot sore and weary
they are still quarrelling as i
close i can do no less than
say thank you mable and henry in
advance for mailing this

archy

mehitabel sings a song

well boss mehitabel the cat
has been woong
the muse no pun please
and i am pivileged
to present her song just
as she sang it to
several of her dubious
feline friends in the alley
last night as follows

there s a dance or two
in the old dame yet
believe me you
there s a dance or two
before i m through
you get me pet
there s a dance or two
in the old dame yet

life s too dam funny
for me to explain
it s kicks or money
life s too dam funny
it s one day sunny
the next day rain
life s too dam funny
for me to explain

but toujours gai
is my motto kid

mehitabel sings a song

the devil s to pay
but toujours gai
and once in a way
let s lift the lid
but toujours gai
is my motto kid

thank god i m a lady
and class will tell
you hear me sadie
thank god i m a lady
my past is shady
but wotthehell
thank god i m a lady
and class will tell

a gentleman friend
i met t other day
coaxed me to amend
a gentleman friend
you meet on a bend
is often that way
a gentleman friend
i met t other day

i says to him dearie
i live my own life
of marriage i m leery
i says to him dearie
if you wasn t beery
you wouldn t say wife
i says to him dearie
i live my own life

i says to him bertie
i ll end down the bay
the garbage scow s dirty

mehitabel sings a song

i says to him bertie
but me here and gertie
is both on our way
i says to him bertie
i ll end down the bay

i never sing blue
wotthehell bill
believe me you
i never sing blue
there s a dance or two
in the old dame still
i never sing blue
wotthehell bill

it appears to me boss
that mehitabel is still far
from being the quiet
domestic character you and i
had hoped she might become
                    archy

æsop revised by archy

a wolf met a spring
lamb drinking
at a stream
and said to her
you are the lamb
that muddied this stream
all last year
so that i could not get
a clean fresh drink
i am resolved that
this outrage
shall not be enacted again
this season
i am going to kill you
just a moment
said the lamb
i was not born last
year so it could not
have been i
the wolf then pulled
a number of other
arguments as to why the lamb
should die
but in each case the lamb
pretty innocent that she was
easily proved
herself guiltless
well well said the wolf
enough of argument

you are right and i am wrong
but i am going to eat
you anyhow
because i am hungry
stop exclamation point
cried a human voice
and a man came over
the slope of the ravine
vile lupine marauder
you shall not kill that
beautiful and innocent
lamb for i shall save her
exit the wolf
left upper entrance
snarling
poor little lamb
continued our human hero
sweet tender little thing
it is well that i appeared
just when i did
it makes my blood boil
to think of the fright
to which you have been
subjected in another
moment i would have been
too late come home with me
and the lamb frolicked
about her new found friend
gambolling as to the sound
of a wordsworthian tabor
and leaping for joy
as if propelled by a stanza
from william blake
these vile and bloody wolves
went on our hero
in honest indignation
they must be cleared out

æsop revised by archy

of the country
the meads must be made safe
for sheepocracy
and so jollying her along
with the usual human hokum
he led her to his home
and the son of a gun
did not even blush when
they passed the mint bed
gently he cut her throat
all the while inveighing
against the inhuman wolf
and tenderly he cooked her
and lovingly he sauced her
and meltingly he ate her
and piously he said a grace
thanking his gods
for their bountiful gifts to him
and after dinner
he sat with his pipe
before the fire meditating
on the brutality of wolves
and the injustice of
the universe
which allows them to harry
poor innocent lambs
and wondering if he
had not better
write to the papers
for as he said
for god s sake can t
something be done about it
                    archy

cheerio my deario

well boss i met
mehitabel the cat
trying to dig a
frozen lamp chop
out of a snow
drift the other day

a heluva comedown
that is for me archy
she says a few
brief centuries
ago one of old
king
tut
ankh
amen s favourite
queens and today
the village scavenger
but wotthehell
archy wotthehell
it s cheerio
my deario that
pulls a lady through

see here mehitabel
i said i thought
you told me that
it was cleopatra
you used to be

cheerio my deario

before you
transmigrated into
the carcase of a cat
where do you get
this tut
ankh
amen stuff
question mark

i was several
ladies my little
insect says she
being cleopatra was
only an incident
in my career
and i was always getting
the rough end of it
always being
misunderstood by some
strait laced
prune faced bunch
of prissy mouthed
sisters of uncharity
the things that
have been said
about me archy
exclamation point

and all simply
because i was a
live dame
the palaces i have
been kicked out of
in my time
exclamation point

but wotthehell
little archy wot

cheerio my deario

thehell
it s cheerio
my deario
that pulls a
lady through
exclamation point

framed archy always
framed that is the
story of all my lives
no chance for a dame
with the anvil chorus
if she shows a little
motion it seems to
me only yesterday
that the luxor local
number one of
the ladies axe
association got me in
dutch with king tut and
he slipped me the
sarcophagus always my
luck yesterday an empress
and today too
emaciated to interest
a vivisectionist but
toujours gai archy
toujours gai and always
a lady in spite of hell
and transmigration
once a queen
always a queen
archy
period

one of her
feet was frozen

cheerio my deario

but on the other three
she began to caper and
dance singing it s
cheerio my deario
that pulls a lady
through her morals may
have been mislaid somewhere
in the centuries boss but
i admire her spirit

                    archy

the lesson of the moth

i was talking to a moth
the other evening
he was trying to break into
an electric light bulb
and fry himself on the wires

why do you fellows
pull this stunt i asked him
because it is the conventional
thing for moths or why
if that had been an uncovered
candle instead of an electric
light bulb you would
now be a small unsightly cinder
have you no sense

plenty of it he answered
but at times we get tired
of using it
we get bored with the routine
and crave beauty
and excitement
fire is beautiful
and we know that if we get
too close it will kill us
but what does that matter
it is better to be happy
for a moment
and be burned up with beauty

the lesson of the moth

than to live a long time
and be bored all the while
so we wad all our life up
into one little role
and then we shoot the roll
that is what life is for
it is better to be a part of beauty
for one instant and then chase to
exist than to exist forever
and never be a part of beauty
our attitude towards life
is come easy go easy
we are like human beings
used to be before they became
too civilized to enjoy themselves

and before i could argue him
out of his philosophy
he went and immolated himself
on a patent cigar lighter
i do not agree with him
myself i would rather have
half the happiness and twice
the longevity

but at the same time i wish
there was something i wanted
as badly as he wanted to fry himself
                                    archy

xxi

a roach of the taverns

i went into a
speakeasy the other night
with some of the
boys and we were all sitting
around under one of
the tables making
merry with crumbs and
cheese and what not but
after a while a strange
melancholy descended
upon the jolly crew and
one old brown veteran roach
said with a sigh well
boys eat drink and
be maudlin for
tomorrow we are dry the
shadow of the padlock
rushes toward us
like a sahara sandstorm
flinging itself at an oasis
for years myself and my
ancestors before me have
inhabited yonder ice box but
the day approaches
when our old homestead
will be taken away from
here and scalded out
yes says i soon there will
be nothing but that

a roach of the taverns

eheu fugaces stuff
on every hand i
never drank it says he
what kind of a
drink is it
it is bitter as wormwood
says i and the
only chaser to it is
the lethean water
it is not the booze itself
that i regret so
much said the old brown
roach it is the
golden companionship of
the tavern myself
and my ancestors have been
chop house and tavern
roaches for hundreds of years
countless generations back
one of my elizabethan
forebears was plucked from
a can of ale in the
mermaid tavern by
will shakespeare and
put down kit marlowe s back
what subtle wits they were in
those days said i yes
he said and later
another one of my
ancestors was
introduced into a larded
hare that addison
was eating by dicky steele
my ancestor came
scurrying forth dicky
said is that your own
hare joe or a wig a

a roach of the taverns

thing which addison
never forgave yours is a
remarkable family
history i said yes he
said i am the last
of a memorable
line one of my
ancestors was found drowned
in the ink well
out of which poor
eddie poe wrote the
raven we have
always associated with wits
bohemians and bon
vivants my maternal
grandmother was slain by
john masefield with
a bung starter well well it
is sad i said the
glad days pass yes
he says soon we will all
be as dry as the
egyptian scarab that
lies in the sarcophagus
beside the mummy of rameses and
he hasn t had a
drink for four thousand
years it is sad for
you he continued but
think how much sadder it
is for me with
a family tradition such as
mine only one of my
ancestors cheese it i said
interrupting him i do
not wish to injure
your feelings but i weary

a roach of the taverns

of your ancestors i
have often noticed that
ancestors never boast
of the descendants who boast
of ancestors i would
rather start a family than
finish one blood will tell but often
it tells too much

> archy

the froward ladybug

boss is it not awful
the way some female
creatures mistake ordinary
politeness for sudden
adoration
i met a katydid in a
beef stew in ann
street the other evening her
foot slipped and she
was about to sink
forever when i pushed her a
toothpick since i
rescued her the poor silly
thing follows me about
day and night i always felt
my fate would be a
poet she says to me how lovely
to be rescued by one i
am musical myself my
nature is sensitive to it so
much so that for
months i dwelt in a grand
piano in carnegie hall i
hope you don t think
i am bold no i said you
seem timid to me you
seem to lack courage entirely the
way you dog my footsteps
one would think you

the froward ladybug

were afraid to be alone i do
not wish any one any
ill luck but if
this shrinking thing got
caught in a high wind and
was blown out to
open sea i hope she would
be saved by a ship
outward bound for
madagascar

                    archy

pete the parrot and shakespeare

i got acquainted with
a parrot named pete recently
who is an interesting bird
pete says he used
to belong to the fellow
that ran the mermaid tavern
in london then i said
you must have known
shakespeare know him said pete
poor mutt i knew him well
he called me pete and i called him
bill but why do you say poor mutt
well said pete bill was a
disappointed man and was always
boring his friends about what
he might have been and done
if he only had a fair break
two or three pints of sack
and sherris and the tears
would trickle down into his
beard and his beard would get
soppy and wilt his collar

i remember one night when
bill and ben jonson and
frankie beaumont
were sopping it up

here i am ben says bill
nothing but a lousy playwright

pete the parrot and shakespeare

and with anything like luck
in the breaks i might have been
a fairly decent sonnet writer
i might have been a poet
if i had kept away from the theatre

yes says ben i ve often
thought of that bill
but one consolation is
you are making pretty good money
out of the theatre

money money says bill what the hell
is money what i want is to be
a poet not a business man
these damned cheap shows
i turn out to keep the
theatre running break my heart
slap stick comedies and
blood and thunder tragedies
and melodramas say i wonder
if that boy heard you order
another bottle frankie
the only compensation is that i get
a chance now and then
to stick in a little poetry
when nobody is looking
but hells bells that isn t
    what i want to do
    i want to write sonnets and
    songs and spenserian stanzas
    and i might have done it too
if i hadn t got
into this frightful show game
business business business
grind grind grind
what a life for a man
that might have been a poet

well says frankie beaumont
why don t you cut it bill
i can t says bill
i need the money i ve got
a family to support down in
the country well says frankie
anyhow you write pretty good
plays bill any mutt can write
plays for this london public
says bill if he puts enough
murder in them what they want
is kings talking like kings
never had sense enough to talk
and stabbings and stranglings
and fat men making love
and clowns basting each
other with clubs and cheap puns
and off colour allusions to all
the smut of the day oh i know
what the low brows want
and i give it to them

well says ben jonson
don t blubber into the drink
brace up like a man
and quit the rotten business
i can t i can t says bill
i ve been at it too long i ve got to
the place now where i can t
write anything else
but this cheap stuff
i m ashamed to look an honest
young sonneteer in the face
i live a hell of a life i do
the manager hands me some mouldy old
manuscript and says
bill here s a plot for you

pete the parrot and shakespeare

this is the third of the month
by the tenth i want a good
script out of this that we
can start rehearsals on
not too big a cast
and not too much of your
damned poetry either
you know your old
familiar line of hokum
they eat up that falstaff stuff
of yours ring him in again
and give them a good ghost
or two and remember we gotta
have something dick burbage can get
his teeth into and be sure
and stick in a speech
somewhere the queen will take
for a personal compliment and if
you get in a line or two somewhere
about the honest english yeoman
it s always good stuff
and it s a pretty good stunt
bill to have the heavy villain
a moor or a dago or a jew
or something like that and say
i want another
comic welshman in this
but i don t need to tell
you bill you know this game
just some of your ordinary
hokum and maybe you could
kill a little kid or two a prince
or something they like
a little pathos along with
the dirt now you better see burbage
tonight and see what he wants
in that part oh says bill

pete the parrot and shakespeare

to think i am
debasing my talents with junk
like that oh god what i wanted
was to be a poet
and write sonnet serials
like a gentleman should

well says i pete
bill s plays are highly
esteemed to this day
is that so says pete
poor mutt little he would
care what poor bill wanted
was to be a poet

archy

archy confesses

coarse
jocosity
catches the crowd
shakespeare
and i
are often
low browed

the fish wife
curse
and the laugh
of the horse
shakespeare
and i
are frequently
coarse

aesthetic
excuses
in bill s behalf
are adduced
to refine
big bill s
coarse laugh

but bill
he would chuckle
to hear such guff
he pulled

archy confesses

rough stuff
and he liked
rough stuff

hoping you
are the same
                archy

the old trouper

i ran onto mehitabel again
last evening
she is inhabiting
a decayed trunk
which lies in an alley
in greenwich village
in company with the
most villainous tom cat
i have ever seen
but there is nothing
wrong about the association
archy she told me
it is merely a plutonic
attachment
and the thing can be
believed for the tom
looks like one of pluto s demons
it is a theatre trunk
archy mehitabel told me
and tom is an old theatre cat
he has given his life
to the theatre
he claims that richard
mansfield once
kicked him out of the way
and then cried because
he had done it and
petted him
and at another time

the old trouper

he says in a case
of emergency
he played a bloodhound
in a production of
uncle tom s cabin
the stage is not what it
used to be tom says
he puts his front paw
on his breast and says
they don t have it any more
they don t have it here
the old troupers are gone
there s nobody can troupe
any more
they are all amateurs nowadays
they haven t got it
here
there are only
five or six of us oldtime
troupers left
this generation does not know
what stage presence is
personality is what they lack
personality
where would they get
the training my old friends
got in the stock companies
i knew mr booth very well
says tom
and a law should be passed
preventing anybody else
from ever playing
in any play he ever
played in
there was a trouper for you
i used to sit on his knee
and purr when i was

103

the old trouper

a kitten he used to tell me
how much he valued my opinion
finish is what they lack
finish
and they haven t got it
here
and again he laid his paw
on his breast
i remember mr daly very
well too
i was with mr daly s company
for several years
there was art for you
there was team work
there was direction
they knew the theatre
and they all had it
here
for two years mr daly
would not ring up the curtain
unless i was in the
prompter s box
they are amateurs nowadays
rank amateurs all of them
for two seasons i played
the dog in joseph
jefferson s rip van winkle
it is true i never came
on the stage
but he knew i was just off
and it helped him
i would like to see
one of your modern
theatre cats
act a dog so well
that it would convince
a trouper like jo jefferson

the old trouper

but they haven t got it
nowadays
they haven t got it
here
jo jefferson had it he had it
here
i come of a long line
of theatre cats
my grandfather
was with forrest
he had it he was a real trouper
my grandfather said
he had a voice
that used to shake
the ferryboats
on the north river
once he lost his beard
and my grandfather
dropped from the
fly gallery and landed
under his chin
and played his beard
for the rest of the act
you don t see any theatre
cats that could do that
nowadays
they haven t got it they
haven t got it
here
once i played the owl
in modjeska s production
of macbeth
i sat above the castle gate
in the murder scene
and made my yellow
eyes shine through the dusk
like an owl s eyes

the old trouper

modjeska was a real
trouper she knew how to pick
her support i would like
to see any of these modern
theatre cats play the owl s eyes
to modjeska s lady macbeth
but they haven t got it nowadays
they haven t got it
here

mehitabel he says
both our professions
are being ruined
by amateurs

                              archy

xxxi

archy declares war

i am going to start
a revolution
i saw a kitchen
worker killing
water bugs with poison
hunting pretty
little roaches
down to death
it set my blood to
boiling
i thought of all
the massacres and slaughter
of persecuted insects
at the hands of cruel humans
and i cried
aloud to heaven
and i knelt
on all six legs
and vowed a vow
of vengeance
i shall organize the insects
i shall drill them
i shall lead them
i shall fling a billion
times a billion billion
risen insects in an army
at the throats
of all you humans
unless you sign the papers

archy declares war

for a damn site better treatment
volunteers volunteers
hearken to my calling
fifty million flies
are wanted may the first
to die in marmalade
curses curses curses
on the cruel human race
does not the poor mosquito
love her little offspring
that you swat against the wall
out of equatorial
swamps and fever jungles
come o mosquitoes
a billion billion strong
and sting a billion baldheads
till they butt against each other
and break like egg shells
caterpillars locusts
grasshoppers gnats
vampire moths
black legged spiders
with red hearts of hell
centipedes and scorpions
little gingery ants
come come come
come you tarantulas
with fury in your feet
bloodsuckers wriggle
out of the bayous
ticks cooties hornets
give up your pleasures
all your little trivial
sunday school picnics
this is war
in earnest
and red revolution

archy declares war

come in a cloud
with a sun hiding miracle
of small deadly wings
swarm stab and bite
what we want is justice
curses curses curses
over land air and water
whirl in a million
sweeping and swaying
cyclonic dances
whirl high and swoop
down on the cities
like a comet bearing death
in the loop and flick
of its tail
little little creatures
out of all your billions
make great dragons
that lie along the sky
and war with the sunset
and eat up the moon
draw all the poison
from the evil stars
and spit it on the earth
remember every planet
pivots on an atom
and so you are strong
i swear by the great
horned toad of mithridates
i swear by the vision
of whiskered old pythagoras
that i am very angry
i am mad as hell
for i have seen a soapy
kitchen mechanic
murdering my brothers
slaying little roaches

archy declares war

pathetic in their innocence
damn her red elbows
damn her spotted apron
damn her steamy hair
damn her dull eyes
that look like a pair
of little pickled onions
curses curses curses
i even heard her praised
for undertaking murder
on her own volition
and called the only perfect
cook in the city
come come come
come in your billions
tiny small feet
and humming little wings
crawlers and creepers
wigglers and stingers
scratchers borers slitherers
little forked tongues
man is at your mercy
one sudden gesture
and all his empires perish
rise
strike for freedom
curses on the species
that invented roach poison
curses on the stingy
beings that evolved
tight zinc covers
that you can t crawl under
for their garbage cans
come like a sandstorm
spewed from the mouth
of a great apocalyptic
desert making devil

archy declares war

come like the spray
sooty and fiery
snorted from the nostrils
of a sky eating ogre
let us have a little
direct action is the
sincere wish of

          archy

the hen and the oriole

well boss did it
ever strike you that a
hen regrets it just as
much when they wring her
neck as an oriole but
nobody has any
sympathy for a hen because
she is not beautiful
while every one gets
sentimental over the
oriole and says how
shocking to kill the
lovely thing this thought
comes to my mind
because of the earnest
endeavour of a
gentleman to squash me
yesterday afternoon when i
was riding up in the
elevator if i had been a
butterfly he would have
said how did that
beautiful thing happen to
find its way into
these grimy city streets do
not harm the splendid
creature but let it
fly back to its rural
haunts again beauty always

the hen and the orole

gets the best of
it be beautiful boss
a thing of beauty is a
joy forever
be handsome boss and let
who will be clever is
the sad advice
of your ugly little friend
                    archy

xxxiii

ghosts

you want to know
whether i believe in ghosts
of course i do not believe in them
if you had known
as many of them as i have
you would not
believe in them either
perhaps i have been
unfortunate in my acquaintance
but the ones i have known
have been a bad lot
no one could believe in them
after being acquainted with them
a short time
it is true that i have met
them under peculiar
circumstances
that is while they
were migrating into the
bodies of what human beings
consider a lower order
of creatures
before i became a cockroach
i was a free verse poet
one of the pioneers of the artless art
and my punishment for that
was to have my soul
enter the body of a cockroach
the ghosts i have known

ghosts

were the ghosts of persons
who were waiting for a vacant
body to get into
they knew they were going
to transmigrate into the bodies of
lizards lice bats snakes
worms beetles mice alley cats
turtles snails tadpoles
etcetera
and while they were waiting
they were as cross as all get out
i remember talking to one of them
who had just worked his way
upward again he had been in the
body of a flea and he was going
into a cat fish
you would think he might be
grateful for the promotion
but not he
i do not call this much of an advance
he said why could i not
be a humming bird or something
kid i told him it will
take you a million years to work your
way up to a humming bird
when i remember he said
that i used to be a hat check boy
in a hotel i could
spend a million years weeping
to think that i should come to this
we have all seen better days i said
we have all come down in the world
you have not come down as far
as some of us
if i ever get to be a hat check boy
again he said i will sting
somebody for what i have had to suffer

ghosts

that remark will probably cost you
another million years among
the lower creatures i told him
transmigration is a great thing
if you do not weaken
personally my ambition is to get
my time as a cockroach shortened for
good behaviour and be promoted
to a revenue officer
it is not much of a step up but
i am humble
i never ran across any of this
ectoplasm that sir arthur
conan doyle tells of but it sounds
as if it might be wonderful
stuff to mend broken furniture with

                                    archy

archy hears from mars

at eleven o clock
p m on last saturday evening
i received the following
message on my
own private radio set
good evening little archibald
and how are you
this is mars speaking
i replied at once
whom or who
as the case may be
do i know on mars
every one here is familiar
with your work archy
was the answer
and we feel well repaid
for all the trouble we have had
in getting in touch
with your planet
thank you i replied
i would rather hear
mars say that
than any other planet
mars has always been
one of my favourite planets
it is sweet of you
to think that way about us
said mars
and so we continued to pay
117

archy hears from mars

each other interstellar
compliments
what is or are
thirty five million miles
between kindred souls
tell us all about
your planet said mars
well i said it is
round like an orange
or a ball
and it is all cluttered
up with automobiles
and politicians
it doesn t know where it is
going nor why
but it is in a hurry
it is in charge of a
two legged animal called
man who is genuinely
puzzled as to whether
his grandfather was a god
or a monkey
i should think said mars
that what he is himself
would make more difference
than what his grandfather was
not to this animal i replied
he is the great alibi ike of
the cosmos when he raises hell
just because he feels like
raising hell
he wants somebody to blame it on
can t anything be done about him
said mars
i am doing the best i can
i answered
but after all i am only one

archy hears from mars

and my influence is limited
you are too modest archy
said mars
we all but worship you
here on this planet
a prophet said i is not
without honour save on his own
planet wait a minute
said mars
i want to write that down
that is one of your best things
archy is it original
it was once i answered truthfully
and may be again
won t you tell us a little
something said mars
about yourself what you look like
and what you think
is the best thing you have written
and your favourite games
and that sort of thing
well i said i am brunette
and stand over six feet
without any shoes on
the best skits i have done
were some little plays
i dashed off
under the general title
of shakespeare s plays
and my favourite sport is theology
you must meet
a great many interesting people
said mars
oh yes i said one becomes
accustomed to that after a while
what is your favourite dish
said mars and do you believe

archy hears from mars

in the immortality of the soul
stew i said and yes
at least mine is immortal
but i could name several others
that i have my doubts about
is there anything else
of interest about your planet
which you wish to tell your
many admirers on mars
asked mars
there is very little else
of any real interest i said
and now will you tune out
and let me do some work
you people who say you admire
my work are always butting in
and taking up my time
how the hell can i get any
serious literary work done
if you keep bothering me
all the time now you get off
the ether and let me do some
deep thinking
you might add that i am shy
and loathe publicity

                              archy

mehitabel dances with boreas

well boss i saw mehitabel
last evening
she was out in the alley
dancing on the cold cobbles
while the wild december wind
blew through her frozen whiskers
and as she danced
she wailed and sang to herself
uttering the fragments
that rattled in her cold brain
in part as follows

whirl mehitabel whirl
spin mehitabel spin
thank god you re a lady still
if you have got a frozen skin

blow wind out of the north
to hell with being a pet
my left front foot is brittle
but there s life in the old dame yet

dance mehitabel dance
caper and shake a leg
what little blood is left
will fizz like wine in a keg

wind come out of the north
and pierce to the guts within

mehitabel dances with boreas

but some day mehitabel s guts
will string a violin

moon you re as cold as a frozen
skin of yellow banan
that sticks in the frost and ice
on top of a garbage can

and you throw a shadow so chilly
that it can scarcely leap
dance shadow dance
you ve got no place to sleep

whistle a tune north wind
on my hollow marrow bones
i ll dance the time with three good feet
here on the alley stones

freeze you bloody december
i never could stay a pet
but i am a lady in spite of hell
and there s life in the old dame yet

whirl mehitabel whirl
flirt your tail and spin
dance to the tune your guts will cry
when they string a violin

eight of my lives are gone
it s years since my fur was slicked
but blow north wind blow
i m damned if i am licked

girls we was all of us ladies
we was o what the hell
and once a lady always game
by crikey blood will tell

mehitabel dances with boreas

i might be somebody s pet
asleep by the fire on a rug
but me i was always romantic
i had the adventurous bug

caper mehitabel caper
leap shadow leap
you gotto dance till the sun comes up
for you got no place to sleep

i might have been many a tom cat s wife
but i got no regret
i lived my life as i liked my life
and there s pep in the old dame yet

blow wind out of the north
you cut like a piece of tin
slice my guts into fiddle strings
and we ll have a violin

spin mehitabel spin
you had a romantic past
and you re gonna cash in dancing
when you are croaked at last

i will not eat tomorrow
and i did not eat today
but wotthehell i ask you
the word is toujours gai

whirl mehitabel whirl
i once was a maltese pet
till i went and got abducted
and cripes i m a lady yet

whirl mehitabel whirl
and show your shadow how
123

mehitabel dances with boreas

tonight its dance with the bloody moon
tomorrow the garbage scow

whirl mehitabel whirl
spin shadow spin
the wind will pipe on your marrow bones
your slats are a mandolin

by cripes i have danced the shimmy
in rooms as warm as a dream
and gone to sleep on a cushion
with a bellyful of cream

it s one day up and next day down
i led a romantic life
it was being abducted so many times
as spoiled me for a wife

dance mehitabel dance
till your old bones fly apart
i ain t got any regrets
for i gave my life to my art

whirl mehitabel whirl
caper my girl and grin
and pick at your guts with your frosty fee
they re the strings of a violin

girls we was all of us ladies
until we went and fell
and oncet a thoroughbred always game
i ask you wotthehell

it s last week up and this week down
and always the devil to pay
but cripes i was always the lady
and the word is toujours gai
and the word is toujours gai

mehitabel daces with boreas

be a tabby tame if you want
somebody s pussy and pet
the life i led was the life i liked
and there s pep in the old dame yet

whirl mehitabel whirl
leap shadow leap
you gotto dance till the sun comes up
for you got no place to sleep

archy

archy at the zoo

the centipede adown the street
goes braggartly with scores of feet
a gaudy insect but not neat

the octopus s secret wish
is not to be a formal fish
he dreams that some time he may grow
another set of legs or so
and be a broadway music show

oh do not always take a chance
upon an open countenance
the hippopotamus s smile
conceals a nature full of guile

human wandering through the zoo
what do your cousins think of you

i worry not of what the sphinx
thinks or maybe thinks she thinks

i have observed a setting hen
arise from that same attitude
and cackle forth to chicks and men
some quite superfluous platitude

serious camel sad giraffe
are you afraid that if you laugh
those graceful necks will break in half

archy at the zoo

a lack of any mental outlet
dictates the young cetacean s spoutlet
he frequent blows like me and you
because there s nothing else to do

when one sees in the austral dawn
a wistful penguin perched upon
a bald man's bleak and desert dome
one knows tis yearning for its home

the quite irrational ichneumon
is such a fool it s almost human

despite the sleek shark s far flung grin
and his pretty dorsal fin
his heart is hard and black within
even within a dentist s chair
he still preserves a sinister air
a prudent dentist always fills
himself with gas before he drills
                                   archy

the dissipated hornet

well boss i had a
great example of the corrupting
influence of the great
city brought to my notice recently a
drunken hornet blew in here
the other day and sat down in the
corner and dozed and buzzed not a
real sleep you know one of those wakeful
liquor trances with the
fuzzy talk oozing out of it to hear
this guy mumble in his dreams he was right
wicked my name he says is crusty bill
i never been licked and i never will and
then he would go half way asleep
again nobody around here wanted to
fight him and after a while he got
sober enough to know how drunk he had
been and began to cry over it and get
sentimental about himself mine is a wasted
life he says but i had a good
start red liquor ruined me he says and
sobbed tell me your story i
said two years ago he said i was a country
hornet young and strong and handsome i
lived in a rusty rainspout with my
parents and brothers and sisters and all was
innocent and merry often in that happy
pastoral life would we swoop down
with joyous laughter and sting the school

the dissipated hornet

children on the village green but on an evil
day alas i came to the city in a crate
of peaches i found myself in a market
near the water front alone and friendless in the
great city its ways were strange to
me food seemed inaccessible i thought
that i might starve to death as i was buzzing
down the street thinking these gloomy
thoughts i met another hornet
just outside a speakeasy kid he says
you look down in the mouth forget
it kid i will show you how to live without
working how i says watch me he says just
then a drunken fly came crawling out
of the bar room in a leisurely way my new
found friend stung dissected and consumed that fly
that s the way he says smacking his lips
this is the life that was a beer fly
wait and i will get you a cocktail fly this
is the life i took up that life alas the
flies around a bar room get so drunk drinking
what is spilled that they are helpless all a
hornet has to do is wait calmly until
they come staggering out and there is his
living ready made for him at first being
young and innocent i ate only beer flies but
the curse of drink got me the mad life began
to tell upon me i got so i would not eat a
fly that was not full of some strong and heady
liquor the lights and life got me i would
not eat fruits and vegetables any more i scorned
flies from a soda fountain
they seemed flat and insipid to me
finally i got so wicked that i
went back to the country and got six innocent
young hornets and brought them back
to the city with me i started them in the

E   129

the dissipated hornet

business i debauched them and
they caught my flies for me now i am in
an awful situation my six hornets from the
country have struck and set up on their own
hook i have to catch my flies myself
and my months of idleness and
dissipation have spoiled my technique i
can t catch a fly now unless he is dead drunk
what is to become of me alas the curse
of alcoholic beverages especially with each
meal well i said it is a sad story
bill and of a sort only too
common in this day of ours it is he says i
have the gout in my stinger so bad
that i scream with pain every time i spear
a fly i got into a safe place on the
inside of the typewriter and yelled out at him
my advice is suicide bill all the time
he had been pitying himself my sympathy had
been with the flies

archy

xxxviii

unjust

poets are always asking
where do the little roses go
underneath the snow
but no one ever thinks to say
where do the little insects stay
this is because
as a general rule
roses are more handsome
than insects
beauty gets the best of it
in this world
i have heard people
say how wicked it was
to kill our feathered
friends
in order to get
their plumage and pinions
for the hats of women
and all the while
these same people
might be eating duck
as they talked
the chances are
that it is just as discouraging
to a duck to have
her head amputated
in order to become
a stuffed roast fowl
and decorate a dining table

unjust

as it is for a bird
of gayer plumage
to be bumped
off the running board of existence
to furnish plumage
for a lady s hat
but the duck
does not get the sympathy
because the duck
is not beautiful
the only insect
that succeeds in getting
mourned is a moth
or butterfly
whereas every man s
heel is raised against
the spider
and it is getting harder
and harder for spiders
to make an honest living
at that since
human beings have invented
so many ways
of killing flies
humanity will shed poems
full of tears
over the demise of
a bounding doe
or a young gazelle
but the departure of a trusty
camel leaves the
vast majorities
stonily indifferent
perhaps the theory is
that god would not have made
the camel so ugly
if the camel were not wicked

unjust

alas exclamation point
the pathos of ugliness
is only perceived
by us cockroaches of the world
and personally
i am having to stand for a lot
i am getting it double
as you might say
before my soul
migrated into the body
of a cockroach
it inhabited the carcase
of a vers libre poet
some vers libre poets are beautifu
but i was not
i had a little blond moustache
that every one thought was a mistake
and yet since i have died
i have thought of that
with regret
it hung over a mouth
that i found it difficult to keep closed
because of adenoidal trouble
but it would have been better
if i could have kept it closed
because the teeth within
were out of alignment
and were of odd sizes
this destroyed my acoustics
as you might say
my chin was nothing much
and knew it
and timidly shrank
into itself
receding from the battle of life
my eyes were all right
but my eyebrows

were scarcely noticeable
i suppose though that if
i had had noticeable eyebrows
they would have been wrong
somehow
well well not to pursue
this painful subject
to the uttermost and ultimate
wart and freckle
i was not handsome and it hampered
me when i was a human
it militated against me
as a poet
more beautiful creatures could
write verse worse than mine
and get up and recite it
with a triumphant air
and get away with it
but my sublimest ideas
were thought to be a total
loss when people saw
where they came from
i think it would have been
only justice
if i had been sent to inhabit
a butterfly
but there is very little
justice in the universe
what is the use
of being the universe
if you have to be just
interrogation point
and i suppose the universe
had so much really important
business on hand
that it finds it impossible
to look after the details

unjust

it is rushed
perhaps it has private
knowledge to the effect
that eternity is brief
after all
and it wants to get the big
jobs finished in a hurry
i find it possible to forgive
the universe
i meet it in a give and take spirit
although i do wish
that it would consult me at times
please forgive
the profundity of these
meditations
whenever i have nothing
particular to say
i find myself always
always plunging into cosmic
philosophy
or something

                                            archy

the cheerful cricket

i can t see for the
life of me what there is
about crickets that makes people
call them jolly they
are the parrots of the insect race
crying cheer up cheer up
cheer up over and
over again till you want to
swat them i hate one of these
grinning skipping smirking
senseless optimists worse
than i do a cynic or a
pessimist there was
one in here the other day i was
feeling pretty well
and pleased with the world when
he started that confounded
cheer up cheer up cheer up stuff
fellow i said i am
cheerful enough or i was till
a minute ago but you
get on my nerves it s all right
to be bright and merry
but what s the use
pretending you have more
cheerfulness than there is in the
world you sound
insincere to me you insist on
it too much you make

the cheerful cricket

me want to sit in
a tomb and listen to the
screech owls telling
ghost stories to the tree toads i
would rather that i heard a door squeak have
you only one record the sun
shone in my soul today before
you came and you
have made me think of the
world s woe groan
once or i will go mad your
voice floats around the world like
the ghost of a man
who laughed himself to death
listening to funny stories
the boss told i listen to you
and know why shakespeare
killed off mercutio so
early in the play it is only
hamlet that can
find material for five acts
cheer up cheer up cheer up he
says bo i told him i
wish i was the
woolworth tower i would fall
on you cheer up cheer up cheer
up he says again

archy

clarence the ghost

the longer i live the more i
realize that everything is
relative even morality is
relative things you would not do
sometimes you would do other
times for instance i would not consider
it honourable in me as a
righteous cockroach to crawl into a
near sighted man s soup that
man would not have a sporting chance but
with a man with ordinarily good eye
sight i should say it was
up to him to watch his soup himself and
yet if i was very tired and hungry
i would crawl into even a near
sighted man s soup knowing all the
time it was wrong and my necessity would
keep me from reproaching myself too
bitterly afterwards you can
not make any hard and fast rule
concerning the morality of crawling into
soup nor anything else a certain
alloy of expediency improves the
gold of morality and makes
it wear all the longer consider a
ghost if i were a ghost i
would not haunt ordinary people but i
would have all the fun i wanted to with
spiritualists for spiritualists are

clarence the ghost

awful nuisances to ghosts i knew a
ghost by the name of clarence one
time who hated spiritualists with a
great hatred you see said clarence they
give me no rest they have got my
number once one of those psychics gets a
ghost s number so he has to come
when he is called they work him till
the astral sweat stands out in beads
on his spectral brow they seem to think
said clarence that all a spook has to do
is to stick around waiting to dash in
with a message as to whether mrs millionbucks
pet pom has pneumonia or only wheezes
because he has been eating too many
squabs clarence was quite
bitter about it but wait he says till
the fat medium with the red nose
that has my number
passes over and i can get my
clutches on him on equal terms there s
going to be some initiation beside
the styx several of the boys are
sore on him a plump chance i have
don t i to improve myself and pass on
to another star with that medium
yanking me into somebody s parlour to
blow through one of these little tin
trumpets any time of the day or night
honest archy he says i hate the sight of a
ouija board would it be moral he
says to give that goof a bum tip on the
stock market life ain t worth
dying he says if you ve got to fag
for some chinless chump of a psychic
nor death ain t worth living
through would it be moral in me to

clarence the ghost

queer that simp with his
little circle by saying he s got an
anonymous diamond brooch in his pocket
and that his trances are rapidly developing
his kleptomania no clarence i said it
wouldn t be moral but it
might be expedient there s a ghost
around here i have been trying to get
acquainted with but he is shy i think he is
probably afraid of cockroaches

                                    archy

xli

some natural history

the patagonian
penguin
is a most
peculiar
bird
he lives on
pussy
willows
and his tongue
is always furred
the porcupine
of chile
sleeps his life away
and that is how
the needles
get into the hay
the argentinian
oyster
is a very
subtle gink
for when he s
being eaten
he pretends he is
a skink
when you see
a sea gull
sitting
on a bald man s dome
she likely thinks

some natural history

she s nesting
on her rocky
island home
do not tease
the inmates
when strolling
through the zoo
for they have
their finer feelings
the same
as me and you
oh deride not
the camel
if grief should
make him die
his ghost will come
to haunt you
with tears
in either eye
and the spirit of
a camel
in the midnight gloom
can be so very
cheerless
as it wanders
round the room
                    archy

xlii

prudence

i do not think a prudent one
will ever aim too high
a cockroach seldom whips a dog
and seldom should he try

and should a locust take a vow
to eat a pyramid
he likely would wer out his teeth
before he ever did

i do not think the prudent one
hastes to initiate
a sequence of events which he
lacks power to terminate

for should i kick the woolworth tower
so hard i laid it low
it probably might injure me
if it fell on my toe

i do not think the prudent one
will be inclined to boast
lest circumstances unforeseen
should get him goat and ghost

for should i tell my friends i d drink
the hudson river dry
a tidal wave might come and turn
my statements to a lie

                              archy

archy goes abroad

london england
since i have been
residing in westminster
abbey i have learned
a secret that i desire
to pass on to the psychic
sharps it is this
until the body of a human
being perishes utterly
the spirit is not
released from its vicinity
so long as there is any
form left in the physical
part of it the ghost can not go
to heaven or to hell
the ancient greeks
understood this and they
burned the body very often
so that the spirit could
get immediate release
the ancient egyptians
also knew it
but they reacted differently
to the knowledge
they embalmed the body
so that the form would
persist for thousands
of years and the ghost would have
to stick around for a time

archy goes abroad

here in westminster abbey
there are hundreds of
ghosts that have not yet
been released
some of them are able to wander
a few miles away
and some of them cannot
go further than a few hundred
yards from the graves
where the bodies lie
for the most part they make
the best of it
they go out on little
excursions around london
and at night they sit on
their tombs and
tell their experiences
to each other
it is perhaps the most
exclusive club in london
henry the eighth came in
about three o clock this morning
after rambling about
piccadilly for a couple of hours
and i wish i had the
space to report in detail
the ensuing conversation
between him and charles dickens
now and then
a ghost can so influence
a living person that you
might say he had grabbed off
that living person s body and was
using it as his own
edward the black prince
was telling the gang
the other evening

that he had been leading the life
of a city clerk for three weeks
one of those birds
with a top hat and a sack coat
who come floating through
the mist and drizzle
with manuscript cases
under their arms looking unreal
even when they are not animated
by ghosts edward the black prince
who is known democratically
as neddie black here
says this clerk was a mild and
humble wight when he took
him over but he worked
him up to the place where
he assaulted a policeman
saturday night then left him flat
one of the most pathetic
sights however
is to see the ghost of queen
victoria going out every
evening with the ghost
of a sceptre in her hand
to find mr lytton strachey
and bean him it seems she beans
him and beans him and he
never knows it
and every night on the stroke
of midnight elizabeth tudor
is married to walter raleigh by that
eminent clergyman
dr lawrence sterne
the gang pulls a good many
pageants which are written
by ben jonson but i think
the jinks will not be properly

archy goes abroad

planned and staged until
j m barrie gets here
this is the jolliest bunch
i have met in london
they have learned
since they passed over
that appearances and suety
pudding are not all they were
cracked up to be more anon from your little friend
archy

archy at the tomb of napoleon

paris france
i went over to
the hotel des invalides
today and gazed on
the sarcophagus of the
great napoleon
and the thought came
to me as i looked
down indeed it
is true napoleon
that the best goods
come in the smallest
packages here are
you napoleon with
your glorious course
run and here is
archy just in the
prime of his career
with his greatest
triumphs still before
him neither one of us
had a happy youth
neither one of us
was welcomed socially at
the beginning of his
career neither one of
us was considered much
to look at
and in ten thousand years from

archy at the tomb of napoleon

now perhaps what you said and did
napoleon will be
confused with what
archy said and did
and perhaps the burial
place of neither will be
known napoleon looking
down upon you
i wish to ask you now
frankly as one famous
person to another
has it been worth
all the energy
that we expended all the
toil and trouble and
turmoil that it cost us
if you had your life
to live over
again bonaparte would
you pursue the star
of ambition
i tell you frankly
bonaparte that i myself
would choose the
humbler part
i would put the temptation
of greatness aside
and remain an ordinary
cockroach simple
and obscure but alas
there is a destiny that
pushes one forward
no matter how hard
one may try to resist it
i do not need to
tell you about that
bonaparte you know as

archy at the tomb of napoleon

much about it as i do
yes looking at it in
the broader way neither
one of us has been to blame
for what he has done
neither for his great
successes nor his great mistakes
both of us napoleon
were impelled by some
mighty force external to
ourselves we are both to
be judged as great forces of
nature as tools in the
hand of fate rather than as
individuals who willed to
do what we have done
we must be forgiven
napoleon
you and i
when we have been
different from the common
run of creatures
i forgive you as i know
that you would forgive
me could you speak to me
and if you and i
napoleon forgive and
understand each other
what matters it if all
the world else find
things in both of us that
they find it hard
to forgive and understand
we have been
what we have been
napoleon and let them laugh that off
well after an hour or so of

archy at the tomb of napoleon

meditation there i left
actually feeling that i
had been in communion
with that great spirit and
that for once in my
life i had understood and been
understood
and i went away feeling
solemn but likewise
uplifted mehitabel the
cat is missing

                    archy

mehitabel meets an affinity

paris france
mehitabel the cat
has been passing her
time in the dubious
company of
a ragged eared tom cat
with one mean
eye and the other
eye missing whom
she calls francy
he has been the hero
or the victim of
many desperate encounters
for part of his tail
has been removed
and his back has been chewed
to the spine
one can see at a glance
that he is a sneak thief
and an apache
a bandit with long
curved claws
you see his likes hanging
about the outdoor markets
here in paris waiting
their chance to sneak
a fish or a bit
or unregarded meat
of whimpering

mehitabel meets an affinity

among the chair legs at the
sidewalk cafes in the
evenings or slinking
down the gutters of
alleys in the old
quarters of the town
he has a raucous voice
much damaged by the night
air and yet there is a
sentimental wheedling
note in it as well
and yet withal he carries
his visible disgrace with
a jaunty air
when i asked mehitabel
where in the name of st denis
did you pick up that
romantic criminal
in the luxembourg gardens
she replied where
we had both gone to kill
birds he has been showing me
paris he does not
understand english but speak of
him with respect
he is like myself
an example of the truth
of the pythagorean idea
you know that in my body
which is that of a cat
there is reincarnated
the soul of cleopatra
well this cat here
was not always a cat either
he has seen better days
he tells me that once he was
a bard and lived here in paris

mehitabel meets an affinity

tell archy here
something about yourself francy
thus encouraged the
murderous looking animal spoke
and i append a
rough translation of
what he said

tame cats on a web of the persian woof
may lick their coats and purr for cream
but i am a tougher kind of goof
scheming a freer kind of scheme
daily i climb where the pigeons gleam
over the gargoyles of notre dame
robbing their nests to hear them scream
for i am a cat of the devil i am

i ll tell the world i am a hard boiled œuf
i rend the clouds when i let off steam
to the orderly life i cry pouf pouf
it is worth far less than the bourgeois deem
my life is a dance on the edge de l abime
and i am the singer you d love to slam
who murders the midnight anonyme
for i am a cat of the devil i am

when the ribald moon leers over the roof
and the mist reeks up from the chuckling stream
i pad the quais on a silent hoof
dreaming the vagabond s ancient dream
where the piebald toms of the quartier teem
and fight for a fish or a mouldy clam
my rival i rip and his guts unseam
for i am a cat of the devil i am

roach i could rattle you rhymes by the ream
in proof of the fact that i m no spring lamb

mehitabel meets an affinity

maybe the headsman will finish the theme
for i am a cat of the devil i am

mehitabel i said
your friend is nobody else
than francois villon
and he looks it too

                  archy

mehitabel sees paris

paris france
i have not been
to geneva but i have been
talking to a french cockroach
who has just returned
from there travelling all the
way in a third class
compartment he says there is no
hope for insect or man in
the league of nations
what prestige it ever had is gone
and it never had any
the idea of one great brotherhood
of men and insects on earth
is very attractive to me
but mehitabel the cat
says i am a communist an
anarchist and a socialist
she has been shocked to the soul
she says by what the
revolutionists did here during
the revolution
i am always the aristocrat archy
she said i may go and play
around montmartre and that sort
of thing and in fact i was
playing up there with francy last
night but i am always the lady
in spite of my little larks

mehitabel sees paris

toujours gai archy and toujours
the lady that is my motto in
spite of
ups and downs
what they did to us aristocrats
at the time of the revolution
was a plenty archy
it makes my heart bleed
to see signs of it all
over town those poor
dear duchesses that got it
in the neck i can sympathize
with them archy i may not
look it now but i come of a
royal race myself
i have come down in the world
but wotthehell archy wotthehell
jamais triste archy jamais triste
that is my motto
always the lady and always
out for a good time
francy and i lapped up
a demi of beer in a joint
up on the butte last night
that an american tourist
poured out for us
and everybody laughed and it
got to be the fashion up there
to feed beer to us cats
i did not get a vulgar souse
archy no lady gets a vulgar
souse wotthehell i hope i am above
all vulgarity but i did get a
little bit lit up
and francy did too we came
down and got on top of the
new morgue and sang and did

157

mehitabel sees paris

dances there
francy seems to see
something attractive about
morgues when he gets lit up
the old morgue he says was
a more romantic morgue but
vandal hands have torn it down
but wotthehell archy this one
will do to dance on
francy is showing me a side of
paris he says tourists don t often
get a look at he has a little
love nest down in the
catacombs where
he and i are living now
he and i go down there
and do the tango amongst the
bones he is really a most
entertaining and agreeable
companion archy and he has some
very quaint ideas he is busy now
writing a poem about
us two cats filled with beer
dancing among the bones
sometimes i think francy
is a little morbid
when i see these lovely old places
that us aristocrats built archy
in the hands of the bourgeois it
makes me almost wild
but i try to bear up i try
to bear up i find agreeable
companions and put a good face
on it toujours gai that is my
motto toujours gai
francy is a little bit done up
today he tried to steal a

mehitabel sees paris

partridge out of a frying
pan in a joint up on the butte
we went back there for more beer
after our party
at the morgue
and the cook beaned him with
a bottle poor francy i
should hate to lose him
but something tells me i should
not stay a widow long
there is something in the air
of paris archy
that makes one young again
there s more than one
dance in the old dame yet
and with these words she
put her tail in the air and
capered off down the alley
i am afraid we shall never
get mehitabel back to america

archy

mehitabel in the catacombs

paris france
i would
fear greatly for the morals
of mehitabel the cat if she had any
the kind of life she
is leading is too violent
and undisciplined for words
she and the disreputable
tom cat who claims to have
been francois villon
when he was on earth
before have taken up their
permanent abode in the catacombs
whence they sally
forth nightly on excursions
of the most undignified nature
sometimes they honour
with their presence the cafes
of montparnasse and the boul mich
and sometimes they
seek diversion in the cabarets
on top of the butte
of montmartre
in these localities
it has become the fashion
among the humans
to feed beer to these
peculiar cats and they dance
and caper when they have

mehitabel in the catacombs

become well alcoholized
with this beverage
swinging their tails and
indulging in raucous feline
cries which they evidently
mistake for a song
it was my dubious
privilege to see them
when they returned to their
abode early yesterday morning
flushed as you might say
with bocks and still
in a holiday mood
the catacombs of paris are
not lined with the bones
of saints and martyrs
as are those of rome
but nevertheless these cats
should have more respect
for the relics of mortality
you may not believe me
but they actually danced and
capered among
the skeletons while the cat
who calls himself
francois villon gave forth
a chant of which the following
is a free translation

outcast bones from a thousand biers
click us a measure giddy and gleg
and caper my children dance my dears
skeleton rattle your mouldy leg
this one was a gourmet round as a keg
and that had the brow of semiramis
o fleshless forehead bald as an egg
all men s lovers come to this

mehitabel in the catacombs

this eyeless head that laughs and leers
was a chass daf once or a touareg
with golden rings in his yellow ears
skeleton rattle your mouldy leg
marot was this one or wilde or a wegg
who dropped into verses and down the abyss
and those are the bones of my old love meg
all men s lovers come to this

these bones were a ballet girl s for years
parbleu but she shook a wicked peg
and those ribs there were a noble peer s
skeleton rattle your mouldy leg

and here is a duchess that loved a yegg
with her lipless mouth that once drank bliss
down to the dreg of its ultimate dreg
all men s lovers come to this

prince if you pipe and plead and beg
you may yet be crowned with a grisly kiss
skeleton rattle your mouldy leg
all men s lovers come to this

archy

xlviii

off with the old love

paris france
i think
mehitabel the cat and the
outcast feline
who calls himself francois
villon are about to
quarrel and separate
mehitabel is getting tired
of living in the catacombs
she said to me
last evening
archy i sometimes wish
that francy s gaiety
did not so frequently take
a necrological turn
when francy is really happy
he always breaks
into a series of
lyric epitaphs
personally archy
i am a lady who can
be gay outside of
a mausoleum
as for morgues
and cemeteries i can
take them or i can
leave them alone
just because some of my
ancestors are now mummies.

off with the old love

i do not feel
that i have to wait
till i see a sarcophagus
before i cheer up
i can fall in love
with a gentleman friend without
speculating how he is going
to look to the undertaker
and when i want to sing
a comic song
i do not always feel
impelled to hunt up a tomb
for a stage
i am a lady of refinement
archy i have had my ups
and downs and i have made
a few false steps in life
but i am toujours la grande dame
archy always the lady
old kid to hell with anything
coarse or unrefined
that has always been my motto
and the truth is that this
francy person has a yellow
streak of commonness
running through his poetic nature
i fell for him archy
but i feel there is trouble
coming we had words last
night over something no real
gentleman would have noticed
and the slob said to me
mehitabel if you make eyes again
at that tortoise shell
cat over there i will slice
your eyes out
with a single sweep of claws

and toss them to the pigeons
archy those are words
that no gentleman would use
or no lady would take
you piebald fish thief
i told him
if i were not too refined
i would rip you
from the gullet to the mid riff
it is lucky for you
you frog eating four flush
that i always remember
my breeding
otherwise you would be
a candidate for what they call
civet stew in paris
something I won t stand for in a
gentleman friend
is jealousy of every other
person who may be attracted to me
by my gaiety and
aristocratic manner
and if i hear another word
out of you
i will can you first
and kill you afterwards
and then i will ignore you
archy a gentleman
with any real spirit
would have swung on me
when i said that
but this quitter let me
get away with it
i clawed him a little archy
just to show him i could
and the goof stood for it
no cat can hold me archy

off with the old love

that lets me claw him without
a come back i am a strong free
spirit and i live my own
life and only a masterful
cave cat can hold my affections
he must be a gentleman
but he must also make me feel
that he could be a
wild cat if he would
this francy person is neither
one nor the other
ah me archy i am afraid
my little romance
is drawing to a close
and no meal ticket in sight
either but what the hell archy
a lady can always find friends
it won t be the first time
i have been alone in the world
toujours gai archy
that is my motto
there s more than one dance
in the old dame yet

                              archy

the end